The Expert in the Room

Drive Raving Fans to Your Business with a Book, Even If You Hate Writing

Christopher Robin Roel

Income Disclaimer

This document contains business strategies, marketing methods and other business advice that, regardless of my own results and experience, may not produce the same results (or any results) for you. I make absolutely no guarantee, expressed or implied, that by following the advice below you will make any money or improve current profits, as there are several factors and variables that come into play regarding any given business.

Primarily, results will depend on the nature of the product or business model, the conditions of the marketplace, the experience of the individual, and situations and elements that are beyond your control.

As with any business endeavor, you assume all risk related to investment and money based on your own discretion and at your own potential expense.

Liability Disclaimer

By reading this document, you assume all risks associated with using the advice given below, with a full understanding that you, solely, are responsible for anything that may occur as a result of putting this information into action in any way, and regardless of your interpretation of the advice.

You further agree that our company cannot be held responsible in any way for the success or failure of your business as a result of the information presented below. It is your responsibility to conduct your own due diligence regarding the safe and successful operation of your business if you intend to apply any of our information in any way to your business operations.

Terms of Use

You are given a non-transferable, "personal use" license to this product. You cannot distribute it or share it with other individuals.

Also, there are no resale rights or private label rights granted when purchasing this document. In other words, it's for your own personal use only.

*For my 5th grade teacher Mrs. Bennett...who
encouraged me to start
writing...*

Table of Contents

The Expert in the Room

Drive Raving Fans to Your Business with a Book, Even If You Hate Writing

Introduction

Every business person needs a book. Entrepreneurs, Youtubers, real estate agents, personal trainers, digital marketers, and the list goes on and on. Anyone who stands in front of people and speaks needs to add a book to their sales funnel. It IS...the ultimate business card.

Yes you can earn millions in passive royalties over time, but for what I am going to show you, there's more money in the back end. The "book" is going to make you...the Expert in the Room.

It is going to build your credibility and make people want to buy from you, and more of it. They're going to trust you and ultimately become your raving fan. But don't worry. You won't have to spend thousands buying inventory of your book to sit in you mom's attic. Even if you hate writing, I'm going to show you the way of the future to be an published author...and hopefully a "best selling author". Thanks to technology and POD (print on demand) services, publishing a book has become easier and cheaper than ever.

In the pages ahead, I am going to walk you through the secrets and show you that even if you hate writing, you NEED to publish a book and send raving fans to your business, site, blog, or email list.

Don't worry. Do you think that people like Donald Trump, Oprah, and Tony Robins have time to punch keys. Maybe they do, but it's not time effective. Their time is way more valuable spent doing other more productive tasks.

I'm going to cover how to get it done for pennies on the dollar, and not waste your valuable time.

Who am I?
Before we get started let me briefly introduce myself. I'm Christopher Robin Roel...yes my mother named me that. Ha! I am a 5 time best selling author, with 1,000s of downloads all over the world (under my short name, Chris Roel).

I published my first book in 2014, when I was trying become an authority in the Bully Proof niche to send interested parents to my Brazilian Capoeira dojo. My second book, Ginga and Roll Strong, hit #1 on Amazon and I was just ecstatic. Since then, I hit number one several more times and even with digital products that were priced at $47.99 outselling cheaper competitors priced at $2.99.

The martial arts and fitness niches are my passions, but then I started publishing books for clients. All inclusive book packages, where all they had to do was have one or two meetings with me and then I handed them fully published physical and digital book.

I loved it! Watching them become published authors, and feeding their business hungry leads is an amazing experience. Follow me in the pages ahead, and I'll explain exactly how it'll do the same for you and turn you into the Expert in the Room.

Chapter One
Why You Should Self-Publish Now

Amazon has over 350 million credit card numbers on file for one-touch buying, and growing. Can you imagine just 1% of that looking to buy a book in your niche? I think you can draw the conclusion on that one. Amazon will also spend their own money to run retargeting ads on Google and Facebook for your book.

Most publishers and writers I know don't even do that for themselves. They are going to do email retargeting for your book. Have you ever been browsing on Amazon and then you get an email later that day that suggests similar products and books? Of course you have. Amazon don't play.

And that's why I'm going to show you one business model for harnessing the power the Amazon and online traffic to send cus-tomers to your lead list, and ultimately to your buyer list. There are several online business models with similar strategies and techniques, but let's keep it simple.

You are in the (enter your niche) business, and you don't need to be overwhelmed with a bunch of new technical jargon. As you start learning these new skills, we can pour on heavier sauce in due time.

Instant Credibility

When potential clients know that you are a published author, or even a best selling author, they instantly trust you. This isn't some type of scam, you gotta know your stuff, but...having that published book or books reinforces your professionally.

There's less effort trying to convince some-body that you are who you say you are. They know you are because they read your book, or know about your book. There is still a lot of belief that publishing is a big deal, and you must be pretty serious about what you do to have one.

Attract Your Ideal Clients

I know that we have all been there. Wast-ing your time trying to sell your product or service to a person who doesn't want it. Why the hell were they even talking to you? Could they even afford what your selling? This type thing happens all the time to sales and business people. There was a break down in where they were fishing for leads. The old way of sales was, "hit the yellow pages and dial".

That antiquated way bred a low conversion rate and made people hate sales and salespeople. Since Google and Facebook, have made leaps and bounds in targeting people who want your product, the landscape will never be the same.

You type in "Dog Sitters in San Diego", boom you get sites for Dog Sites in San Diego, plus ads for businesses that dog sit in San Diego, and other places.

You like Martial Arts Movies on Facebook, soon you will get ads for your local MMA gym and kids' karate lessons. But the difference between Google and Amazon as search engines is the point I made at the beginning of this chapter...**350 million credit card numbers on file.**

Amazon is the most trusted website on the planet. When people search on Google they want information and possibly directions. When they go to Amazon, they go to buy.

It's that simple. People are buying e-books and physical books by the millions on Amazon daily. There's a big misconception that people are reading less nowadays. That's absolutely not true.

The reading model has changed, and since the invention of e-readers like the kindle and nook, it has made book buying even easier. People are reading more this day and age, but they're reading shorter books. The 300-450 page book reader still exists, but there are more100-200 page book readers, and even the 50-75 page book reader also.

I'm not talking about Dr. Seuss, either. Real books by legitimate authors, with real valuable information in them....no fluff. What does this all mean for you and the rest of us entrepreneurs?

Real people searching for information on you business niche searching by the hordes on Amazon and other sites will find your book, buy it, read it, and want more of your services.

Even if they don't read it all, or any of it for that matter, they already have a strong feeling of wanting to work with you somehow, buy your products. That initial information session that you have with a client when you first meet already happens in your book.

It does that for you while you sleep, 24 hours a day, 365 days a year. When that person who bought your book and read it, first approaches you...they are primed and ready to buy. All they need to know is how...the ideal customer.

Multiple Streams of Income

Yes, Amazon will direct deposit your royalties from your physical and electronic book sales in your bank account monthly like clockwork. Once you capture their information in a technique I show you later in the book, you can market to them indefinitely. If you are doing what your supposed to which is maintaing contact with them, most of them will buy products and services willingly with little to no resistance.

The old way of making multiple steams of income was owning real estate, making investments, stocks, and whatever business you were in for you main income. That's still legitimate, but now there is kindle royalties, physical book royalties, digital product sales, affiliate partners royalties, coaching, and more.

These aren't small fries either. Some marketers make millions on this alone with no brick and mortar business. An invisible business that can be operated from anywhere in the world. Sound interesting?

I'm not saying to quit your business, but how about adding the digital plan to your current business model, meanwhile sending you hot leads for your main business? Yup. I thought so too.

Be the Expert in the Room

Someone with a book is looked at as an expert in that field. If you are reading this book , I know that you have a lot of experience in what you do...whether it's Yoga, dog walking, water treatment systems, oil and gas, real estate, or whatever you do.

You have the years of experience that show when you talk to someone about it. You can explain every detail inside and out. When some talks about building a home, they will think John Smith, wrote a book on it. He's the expert, let's listen to him...let's buy from him.

When they talk about time management, they will think about Liza Adams. She wrote a book on it. She's the expert. Let's talk to her...let's buy from her.

When they talk about real estate, they will think about Eric Walters. He wrote a book on it. He's the expert...etc. etc.

You get the point. What will they say about you?

Chapter 2
The Order of Value of Your Services

The great Russell Brunson, creator of Clickfunnels and successful internet marketer, wrote in his book Dot Com Secrets the concept of the value ladder. This concept is not new, but let me review it just to make sure that we're all on the same page.

The most expensive you sell should be your time: coaching, services, consulting, etc. Most people/businessmen/entrepreneurs only have one set of products...their services. This is the order of cost or value of your products you should have in this era of the internet.

1. Your digital lead magnate, book, or intro video series.
2. The next expensive or valuable product could be a video training course, E-book or E-course.
3. Group coaching or Group advising, either in your facility or online.
4. Your personal time. One on one coaching or services. Add published author to your

name, or even Best Selling Author, and you can raise this hourly rate, or even charge a retainer for hundreds or thousands of dollars depending on your niche.

Let me give you an example one way a book is going to fit into your funnel in relation to the value of services.

I have a client named Liza. She is a passionate speaker, who works with the city as a trainer. She is constantly giving speeches and training employees. She's super smart and very charismatic. Her peers, colleagues, and followers love her.

She does an awesome presentation on Power Productivity and how to manage time more effectively. Whether her speeches are paid or free, that doesn't matter. If she's giving a free speech, she can use her book as the basis of the speech. She can wave it around the stage and use it as a prop. This instantly builds more credibility and makes her the expert in the room.

At the end of the speech, if she's done her job, she can sell her book at the back of the room for $10-$20. A few hundred extra bucks for her speech...not bad. She can also sell her power productivity write-in journal for $20-$30, because these are generally more expensive to produce. That's another few hundred dollars...still not bad.

Here's where it gets interesting. If she has her digital training products ready to sell, these are generally priced $197-$597, and more. She can make potentially a $12,000 smash and grab speaking for a small group of 20 people.

Then...you guessed it, her coaching services come next. They're a generally people at these events who don't have the time to go over her video training course. They don't have the time to read her awesome book. They do have the money, however, to hire her for her coaching and training services. The most valuable and expensive product she sells. So you see how this value ladder thingy works? Good.

Yes, you have to consider conversion, connection with the audience, pace, and selling from the stage skills, but if she didn't have those products available, guess how much she makes from giving an awesome speech? That's right, double goose eggs! oo

Some people may think that it won't work in their niche. I've seen it done successfully in many niches ranging from dog walking to fitness studios. Let me show you another another example of how it works for another one of my clients...my brother.

I published a book for my brother. His main business is custom home building and real estate brokerage. I published a book for him, "Ten Tips to Build Your Dream Home". People searching for information on how to build their home instead of buying a pre-built home find his book on Amazon, the most trusted website on the planet.
After reading his super valuable, super simple, easy to read 80-page book, they opt in for a free gift in the back of the book.

He offers a free report on how to raise your credit score, and free consultation.

The readers that opt in that live in the service area, are immediately contacted and followed up on to try to offer them services. All subscribers are then sent a drip email sequence giving tips and valuable information, following up with a pitch every 4 emails.

The ones that can afford his services, buy from him. The one's that think it's too much hassle buy another house through his real estate company. Win. Win.

There are many ways to slice it. My brother also has physical copies of his book in his office. When he meets a potential client, he gives them a FREE copy of his book and they are blown away.

Just the fact that he's a published author sets him apart from the other thousands of home builders in the city. The cost of the book is negligible compared to $200-$500 thousand dollar houses he sells. It's the "Ultimate Business Card".

Oh, and if you think my brother likes to write, he doesn't. He doesn't have time to punch keys just like Donald Trump and Tony Robbins doesn't. I'll show you in a later chapter how we get around this and make you a published author.

So, remember the order of value of your services and products. If you don't have any digital and physical products, we'll go over how to create some in a later chapter. See you in the next chapter.

Chapter 3
Build Your Brand

We already discussed my friend and client, Liza. She has a brand and followers that lover her already. Every time she gives a speech, people ask her, "Do you have a book?" Previously she didn't and had to hold her head low in disappointment. That's when she approached me and bought my Turnkey Publish home training course.

Weeks went by and turned into months, and I followed up with her, asking her how the book was coming. She said she didn't even watch it. There are many of us out there just like this. We have kids, businesses, spouses, and other group obligations, like church, Toastmasters, leadership, etc.

That doesn't change the fact that you need to maintain and build your brand with a book or book series. You won't regret it. There's a Youtuber named Mike Vestil. He's probably about 25 years old and he makes goofy videos how to get 6-pack abs, how to get chicks, how to get followers on Youtube, etc. Even this guy knows that he needs a book.

He gives it away for free to get followers on his list, and ultimately sell them digital training products. He lives in Bali in a giant house where he continues to make Youtube videos and live the digital nomad lifestyle.

He is just one of many Youtubers doing the same thing and raking in the doe. Youtube pays them for having so many followers and watch time. Then they further monetize it by selling their books, tee shirts, and other products to raving fans.

It's all about the brand. There are so many of the same products out there. Coke, Pepsi, Nike, Reebok, Nintendo, Xbox, it doesn't really matter how many. After building your following people like you. They want to buy from you. You already have a relationship with them. You have already given them so much value. To the people shaking their heads right now, let me tell you this.

You have expertise that nobody else has. You have your own story that nobody else has. You just have to put yourself out there, be honest, give massive value, and take massive action! The rest will take care of itself.

If you are a personal trainer who lost 60 pounds and turned your life around, people will resonate with that and want to hear more from you.

It happens all over the world in all countries, and even in micro communities. There tons of karate studios, law firms, and real estate companies making money in the same community. They have built their brand and create loyal followers. You can too. You just have to get started, and don't stop once you start.

Imagine your book selling on Amazon to people all over the world. I have followers in India, Australia, Eastern and Western

Europe, the UK and North Africa. I also have followers in Brazil, the home country of the art I teach! Wow. Yes I have some haters. That's what happens when you put yourself out there...especially all over the world. People see you doing good, and want to tear you down.

It's completely normal, and I don't take any of it personal. They're not the ones who are best selling author getting thousands of their books downloaded from all over the world. They're not the ones selling $50-$500 digital products while they sleep.

There's a lot that goes into building your brand: Facebook, Instagram, Amazon, Youtube, Pinterest, Twitter, and others. You have to have your own site and blog. Well, if this seems like a lot of work, you're right. But that's the price to pay build you brand. If you have more money you can pay a digital marketing company to manage your social media. If you have more time, then you can do it yourself, but the fact remains the same.

You have to do it, or you will get left in the digital dust like Toys R'Us and Blockbuster Video.

One way to cut down on your work is to just focus on one or two at a time. You got to know where your target market likes to social on. Older generation like tweeting for some reason. Facebook is becoming older, but is pretty much a mid age range. Instagram and Music.ly are for the middle school to high schoolers, although each has a little bit of everyone.

Find out where your people like to social and focus on that one as your channel. Keeping a blog is a lot of work, although, there is a famous Youtuber named Miles Beckler, who has a great system for creating Youtube videos, turning them into podcasts, blogs, and other media with a very organized method and the help of some apps and the foreign outsource market.

Go check him out. You'll be glad you did. The Youtube channel is one of the fastest growing sites out there, and is the #2 search engine behind Google.

That means that after searching on Google and not finding anything, the average searcher goes right to Youtube and searches there. I do it all the time. Video is growing as the medium of choice and is only going to increase. People want to engage in seeing things right before their very eyes. I know I do. If you don't have a channel on Youtube, you need to get one and put content out on it regularly.

How often? Two to three times a week is what I recommend. Miles Beckler has a great 90 day challenge where he recommends that you make a video every day for 90 days. This really gets the Youtube juice flowing in your favor and gets you followers. But you have to put out valuable content. It's not just some digital algorithmic scam.

Join the future online business model, and leave those naysayers in the dust. Build your brand by whatever channel...but you need a book to go with whatever channels that you are on. See you in the next chapter.

Chapter 4
Publish Your Book, Even if You Hate Writing

Okay let's get to the nitty gritty. I don't want to bog yo down with too much technical speak, so here we go. If you go to the Amazon Kindle website, you can sign up for a free account and upload your manuscript to be published within 24 hours. There are a bunch of little details, however that you need to be aware of, like what you can and can't do. Amazon doesn't like plagiarism. Amazon doesn't like fake reviews, Amazon doesn't like certain book covers. Amazon doesn't like badly edited books.

Amazon is all about the consumer experience. Anything upsetting the buyer will possibly get you banned. The good part is that there are people on Fiverr, Odesk, 99designs, Upwork and many other sites that will help you edit, write, format, illustrate, and even market your book.

I bought my first publishing digital product for $600 that only taught me how to publish books. I was trying to get into publishing after I saw an awesome program by Brian Tracy and Mike Keonigs that was $2000. My wife would have had my heart for dinner if I spent that without telling her.

She wouldn't have let me do it anyway, ha! But I found a cheaper one that was for $600 online, and that I could sneakily buy without her knowing. It was the best decision that I ever made. I improved my brand 1000x, I was able to charge more at my studio, and for private lessons. I started getting speaking gigs, free and paid.

I was able to start creating digital products and profiting through those sales and my book royalties. That was almost 4 years ago from the date of this book. I have hit best seller status 5 times, and am extremely grateful for the decision I made to invest in my personal development. But it would've never happened if I didn't take action.

If you are interested in learning more about my digital training course or full publishing services, I have a gift for you here: http://bit.ly/expertinroom.

Since then I've learned to build funnels online, leverage the title of published author and best selling author, how to create and launch digital products, and how to capture, court, and close email subscribers.

Many people think that seems like you're bugging people to buy stuff, when the opposite is true. People are begging to hear form you, and buy from you. It totally changes the dynamic of cold calling an audience that is not pre-qualified. That's the problem of the old sales methods.

These people read your book, and want more from you. They're opting in on your list because you already did the song and dance with them. They know your expertise already. And the best part is that it happens 24 hours a day while you sleep. Even if you hate writing.

Here is the method that I use for my clients who don't have time to punch keys, or hate writing in general.

We schedule an initial planning meeting to talk about the goals of the book and kick around some ideas. After agreeing on a topic and signing an agreement, we schedule a second interview. We go over the whole book which is outlined and done in question/answer format.

It gets all recorded on an mp3 file. We send it out to a transcriptionist, clean it up, edit it, format it, and buddabing buddaboom, we pop out a book in about 4 weeks. There are also apps, like Trint, that do the transcribing for you. Check it out.

So you see, anyone can be an author. We are living in the future. We can communicate with people around the world with a press of a button. We can hire people in the Philippines for pennies on the dollar.

The organizing and perseverance to carry it through is all you need. We're going to talk about mindset in a later chapter, which is pretty much 90% of being successful.

Let's talk about getting those hungry followers on your list in the first place, because Amazon will not hand over your buyer's emails. They are those most trusted website after all. We will cover the actual email capture system in the next chapter. See you there.

Chapter 5
Build Your Email List Automatically

So how do we get our hungry followers emails when Amazon won't fork em over? Well, you would think they would just give it to you if they are a truly hungry followers, right? Wrong. That's not how it works. I've experimented in many things, but the FREE gift is the best method.

You'll have to test different gifts, as consumers have become more savvy on creepy internet marketers. But when you truly give tons of value, and align the free gift with your target market, the opt-ins should come pouring in. This means you have to know your ideal client avatar.

What the heck is that? The ideal customer avatar, is an exact picture of your ideal client. Someone who loves to throw money at you and your business. Think of him or her. Is it a male or a female. How old are they? What do they drive? Do they have kids? What do they like to read? What podcasts do they listen to? What books do they read? What personalities do they follow? You need to paint an exact picture of your ideal customer, and when writing copy or emails. You write it to them...not a vague list.

For example, my target market is a 35 year old stay at home housewife with two kids. How do I know that? Well, I after being in business for 6 years, I see who gives me the most money, and then I look at the demographics provided on their registration form. My online channel is different. The people that buy my online books, digital products and subscribe to my channels are predominately 35-45 year old men trying to get back in shape.

How do I know that? I use a survey and ask them to fill it out in exchange for a free gift. I made a whole Home Training Course just for this purpose only. I used to get worried about giving away my best material, but I changed my mindset to an abundance mindset. I can always create new products and value. Plus, the information provided in this survey is invaluable. Now I can run ads on Facebook to 35-45 year old out of shape dads in the United States. Boom! Knowledge bomb.

So, go ahead and get started finding out who your ideal customer avatar. The great Ken Spano, successful internet marketer, even names his avatar...like Janet. Ha! It works.

There's also a dynamic of reciprocation that occurs with you and your readers or followers. Once you provide them over-whelming value for free. They really want to know what your paid services are. So I usually always pack my paid products with bonuses worth hundreds extra...for free. I know. I know what you're thinking.

Free? Yup.

You can always create more value and more products, because there will always be more problems to solve, and your fol-lowers will want you to solve them. Trust me. It cost me thousands to learn the in-formation that I am laying out in this book.

I made mistakes, and put in the time publishing, and building funnels, and tweaking my websites, and filming videos, and buying FB ads, and testing all this. This works. You just have to cater it to your business and niche.

So what's the process? Let me give you an example from my Brazilian Capoeira online channel. This is a martial arts fitness niche meaning products can range from $47 to $197. Products in other niches like make money online, self improvement, business coaching, etc. can go for $1,000's.

So take this with a grain a salt. I compiled a few videos from each of my best selling video courses and called it a Home Training Course. I designed a 3D box cover to make it look more professional. Then I started advertising on my Youtube and Facebook channels that I was giving away this course for FREE, as long as the subscribers took my survey and subscribed to my channel.

It worked like gangbusters. There were a few who didn't subscribe and didn't fill out the survey, but it was only like 10% of the opt-ins. Plus I'm not being hard on them. In the survey I asked what other content they wanted to see and what help did they need with their Capoeira. Many beginner Capoeira students don't know what to ask. They don't know enough yet to form questions. They're just taking in all the info, so no problem there.

So now I got their age, sex, experience level, and what products do they want to buy! Likey? Internet marketers are so sneaky...

There are many bulk email management systems like MailChimp, AWeber, Constant Contact, and others. I started out with MailChimp because it was free, but as I was leaning to jump ship, they added free automation! This service which is usually charged for is now free to use for the basic subscriber.

This totally changed the game for me, which now allowed me to send a sequence of emails automatically while I slept. Go check them out if you are just starting out.

As soon as the people click the link on my Youtube channel, or in the back of my book to claim their free gift, they are immediately sent an automatic email something like this:

Hey |First Name of Subscriber|,

Thanks for claiming your free course. Make sure and save this email for your login credentials. Also, make sure you mark this as not Spam, so you can receive my emails. I have a whole bunch of free goodies I'll be sending you over the next few days.

Also, don't forget to subscribe to my Youtube channel here, and take the survey here. I want to know how better to sever you. Let me know if there's anything else I can help you with.

Sincerely,

Christopher Robin Roel

I then schedule a second email 3 days later giving them more valuable advise, and then another 4 days letter. According to Gary Vanyerchuk, he likes using a jab, jab, jab, hook, meaning that you send them three valuable emails first before you pitch a product. People that pitch every email scare off their subscribers, so don't do that.

Also, there is a school of thought that recommends pitching right away as soon as they sign up with a OTO (One time offer) that is too crazy good to pass up. I do that sometimes, with certain funnels, just make sure to test it to see what works best with your audience.

I have like 30 email sequences on autopilot, and you should too. The best time to start your book business was 10 years ago, the second best time is now! So take action.

See you in the next chapter where we'll be talking about a very important topic, "Mindset".

Chapter 6
Mindset

This really should've been chapter one, but I didn't want to scare you off, and I wanted to let you know that this book has tons of value before talking about mumbo jumbo...ha ha! The power of the mind is truly an important topic.

People have self-limiting beliefs that stop them from being successful way before they even try. The Law of Attraction is very popular right no amongst self-help gurus, and internet marketers. The fact is, whatever you think of most naturally attracts itself into your life. But thoughts alone won't get you anywhere.

You have to take massive action! Waiting until the moment is right will leave you waiting forever. You don't have to be great to start, but you have to start to be great. All these popular sayings are true. Miles Beckler has a saying which I have come to like. It's "Fire, Ready, Aim". This means that instead of getting ready to aim, then aiming, then firing, you take action right away. Get your book published. Start your funnel, and then optimize it. I'm not saying put out bad work, but you have to take action even if you think you're not ready.

I was nervous when I released my first book. I had so many doubts and reservations. What if nobody liked it? If I didn't ignore those self-limiting thoughts, I would have never launched my book, nor my second which hit #1 best seller, nor my digital products, website, blog, Youtube channel and publishing business.

Just take action. An influential book I read about 4 years ago is *The Miracle Morning* by Hal Leonard. It details a technique of waking up 1-2 hours earlier than you regularly do, to do a morning ritual to be more productive and improving your life. It really changed my life.

Some of the activities listed in the book were meditation, exercise, writing in your journal and reading. Go check it out. I highly recommend it. Each time I implement a Miracle Morning, I get super productive, and the meditation really improves my daily mindset. You will need a good routine if you want to finish your book in a reasonable amount of time.

Here is my morning routine. I wake up at 5 AM and do thirty minutes of exercise (kicking a punching bag, running, etc.). Then once I get the blood flowing through my body and brain, I do thirty minutes of meditation. I use a guided meditation on Youtube. Some are better, and others aren't so good.

Then I read for thirty minutes. Don't ever stop feeding your brain. You have to become a lifelong learner. Constantly learn new skills, and there are plenty of people who have been there before you. Why wouldn't you want their advice?

The skills I have learned in the last 5 years have benefitted me more than the skills I have learned over the last 20 years. I am learning new things everyday about publishing, best seller strategies, funnels, conversion rates, FB ads, email marketing, design, copywriting, Youtube branding, and more…

Become a lifelong learner.

There is another type of behavior that will prevent you from following through with your book, and I have been guilty of this myself. It's called *shiny object syndrome.*

When I first bought my online self-publishing training, I was engulfed by it. I did nothing else but concentrate on publishing and refining. When I published my second book, a few months later, I went on a buying spree. I bought Internet Marketing Course. I bought a Library Marketing Course. I bought a Digital Products Course.

The problem was that I didn't even give myself time to learn, refine, and master each area before jumping to the next training. I recommend that you concentrate totally on your book until you push it out to launch. Don't buy any other courses. Don't take on any other business ventures. Those will all distract you from your baby...your book and funnel.

On second thought, just concentrate on the book first, then the funnel. Armed with the right mindset, you can persevere through process and come out published author on the other side...and quite possibly best selling author.

You can even use self-affirmations. Look yourself in the mirror and repeat, "I will be a published author" in a serious voice over and over again. You can look up positive daily affirmations on Google, Youtube, or even Amazon. The positive priming of you brain and psyche is very effective. Do not underestimate this simple technique.

There's one last concept I want to talk about before we wrap up this chapter. It's called the Law of Association. It states that whoever you associate with most, you become like.

If you associate with winers, and complacent negative minded people. You, too, will become just like them, and adopt a negative mindset.

If you associate with positive, upbeat, goal orientated people, you will adopt their behavior and mindset becoming upbeat, positive, and goal orientated. There are a lot of people who will try to tear you down, and say that you can't do it. It may be your wife, husband, mother, father, co-worker, best friend, or someone else close to you.

Don't listen. Keep your head up and associate with people who are encouraging, dependable, and hard working. The Law of Association further states that you are an average of your 5 closest friends salaries.

Gary Vanyerchuk said it best.

Get rid of your loser friends and add one winner to your circle every week.

Go to meet ups in your community, mixers, and Masterminds in your city. You will thank yourself ten times over.

Your business will thank you, too. Do you want to scratch in the dirt with the turkeys or fly high like an eagle?

I think you get the point...**Mindset** is key.

Let's get back to taking action. Next up, is digital product creation. See you there.

Chapter 7
Digital Products

We already briefly touched on why you need digital products. I don't think you need anymore convincing right? Good.

What is a digital product? It can be an information product in a PDF document that teaches some sort of valuable information. Even something this simple can sell for $300-$500 depending on what the niches is.

But in reality, video training courses, audio files, mind maps, templates, and regular PDF documents should be used all together. I like to pack my products in with a lot of value. I used to be a high school teacher, and one thing the administration would harp on all the time is that you have to teach to all learning types: visual, auditory, and tactile learners.

It's the same when you are creating a product for you followers. Give them the kitchen sink, stove, and refrigerator. They will be very grateful...plus you can charge more. I host my video training courses on Youtube, but you can use any other video hosting site. Just turn the privacy to unlisted, and embed on your secret linked website.

You can host your cart and sales button on Paypal, but I like to use JVZoo. It integrates Paypal and credit cards, and it's free. It also allows you to build funnels. The craze right now is clickfunnels. It is an all inclusive online software, that has funnel templates, processes payments, and even does auto responder services.

It's not cheap. It ranges from $99-$199/month. The convenience is what you pay for. You don't even need a website, but you can host your domains there if you want.

So, whatever you choose, all you have to do is come up with content, film it, edit it, host it, and then come up with a price. You should do some research at what your competitors are charging if they any products. Don't be too cheap, but you want to price it what it's worth. As long as you pack in the value, your followers will have no problem investing in it. If you are teaching someone to make money with your information, then you can definitely charge more.

Fitness digital products usually peak at a couple hundred bucks, but other niches can go up to $2,000. Remember that publishing program that I passed on? That course is usually packed to the brim, and they launch it a couple times a year.

You don't need a lot of fancy equipment. You can film everything on your Iphone or Galaxy. You will need some editing software, but there's tons of free software that might even come with your computer.

Just make it clean, understandable, and easy to follow. The content is what's most important. You can get a lapel clip microphone on Amazon for $20, which will help clean up your audio, but is not absolutely necessary.

As you create more and more products, you will get the hang of it. Just take action!

Here are some examples of some digital products you can create:

✓6 Pack Abs in 7 Days: Video Training Course
✓How to Make Money in the Stock Market: Step by Step Guide
✓Bitcoin Secrets: Exact Investing Blueprint
✓Dog Walking to Millions: Full Training Course
✓Diet Secrets: Exact Diet Plans that will make you lose 30 pounds

These are just a few examples, but use the Survey Monkey or Google Surveys to find out exactly what your followers want. Whatever you do, don't wait to take action. Learn on the go, or get a coach or mentor to walk you through it. If you're strapped for time, pay someone to do it for you.

Remember, if you have more time do it yourself. If you have more money, pay some to do it for you.

That's exactly what my company does for professionals who don't have time. My clients enjoy the benefits of being a published author with only spending about 3 hours with me. Not bad, ey?

See you in the next chapter where we'll be talking about royalties, series, and pen names.

Chapter 8
Royalties, Series, and Pen Names

I saved this topic for late in the book , because royalties shouldn't be the prime reason you publish a book. You need to be passionate about what you do. Can you make hundreds, thousands, and millions from book royalties? Absolutely, but it takes longer to earn that simply by publishing a book without good marketing.

The way that I have described in this book is more profitable faster. Your book feeds you traffic into your funnel, where digital products are being sold until ultimately followers are buying your services (the most expensive product you have).

There is good news, though. Amazon pays you more royalties than traditional big publishers ever would. At the low end of the scale is %30 royalties from your book sales. Did you think that big publishers are going to give a first time author that much? Think again. Amazon gives you this amount if you price your kindle e-book lower than $2.99 or higher then $9.99. Why? Because they know through data driven research that if you price your book in between$2.99 and $9.99, you will sell more copies.

So they are going to reward you %70 royalties if you price your book in this sweet spot. They make more money. You make more money. Everyone is happy. If you list your book under KDP select, you can also earn royalties whenever someone rents your book, and you get paid for pages read. Pretty cool, right?

These little details took me four years to learn as I navigated through the big Amazon publishing waters. I lay them here at your disposal. Here's another secret most people don't know.

If you list your book under KDP select, you can run free book giveaways and countdown deals. Why would you want to give away your book for free or reduced price? Remember, that the amateur thinks about the front end, while the pros think about the back end. Getting people on your list who are interested in what you got to say, is gold. Targeted free traffic sent from Amazon right to your list.

To use an overused saying from the IM world, "...the money is in the list". It is absolutely true. Are you going to complain about your $2 ebook royalty, when someone enters your list and buys one of your $200 digital products? I didn't think so.

Book Series

Having a series of books is another great way to have your books feed each other. By putting links in the back of your book to your other works, books, and products is a no brainer. After wooing your readers, it is the quickest way to capitalize on a hot buyer.

We still want to capture their email with a FREE gift, but links to your other books in Amazon that can be one-touch-bought is an easy kill, so include both of those in your books.

Pen names

Amazon allows you to have multiple pen names. Niche publishers publish books with different pen names all the time. They want to maintain a certain brand association.

I, for example, write my Capoeira books in my short name Chris Roel. I write my business and publishing books under Christopher Robin Roel, and I have a few other pen names in the kids book niche, and the prepper niche.

The royalties still come rolling into your bank account, so you really have a lot of flexibility in publishing with Amazon. Whether you're branding a specific name with your niche, or you'd rather not be associated with your business, you can always use a pen name.

Many people like to be personality and face of their business, and some do not. They think they are not photogenic, or feel that they'd rather have a better model as the face of their brand. There's nothing wrong with either of those decisions. We'll talk about how to launch your book, once published in the next chapter. See you there.

Chapter 9
The Launch and Launch Team

Okay, you did it. You published your book and now it's up and ready to sell on Amazon. Congratulations! But many authors have books on Amazon that don't sell, and don't even come close to hitting #1 best seller. I've been there.

In one of the frenzies of book publishing I was in, I was releasing book after book without launching them. That was a big mistake.

I'm going to give you a launch model that I use, but there are several others out there. Try this one and see how it works for you. I've hit #1 five times with this model, so it does have a little clout.

Step one is to finish your book and get it approved on Amazon ready to sell. You need your launch team to help you with this one, so either by using KDP's free book giveaway promotion, or by emailing your launch list (75 of your closest friends and colleagues). Let them know that you're releasing your new book and you need reviews. You will give them a free copy in exchange for an honest review. Don't ever buy reviews because Amazon will ban you faster than you can "published".

The number 75 is just a ballpark figure. Get more if you can, but usually 25% of them are going to flake on you. It's just a numbers game. Don't take it personal. After sending out your manuscript, give your team about 2 weeks to read and respond.

Your email list should be super stoked to participate in your new book. They'll feel as if they were apart of the process. Then when you're about to launch the book, change the price from regular price to 0.99 cents. Have all your team buy a copy that day.

Tell your mom and granny. Post it on Facebook, Twitter, and all the other social sites. Let them know that you are having a discounted price for three days only. Run ads on Facebook, Book Buddy, Book Bub, and any other sites you are a member of. Then watch your sales roll in. The Amazon algorithm will work in your favor if everyone is buying at the same. If you have good reviews up, this will help in converting page visitors to buyers.

Watch your Amazon sales rank climb. Hopefully, you can hit #1 like I did. In my home training course and seminars, I detail many other strategies to earn #1 best seller status.

You can even make an event out of it. Have all your launch team over for a launch party. Give them a free copy of your physical book, for buying the kindle version...or not. Every one doesn't have to be in the same room to drive you to number one. It's more about the energy, the vibe, the community surrounding you and your book.

Congrats! You just stepped ahead of your competition by becoming a published author, and hopefully, a best selling author.

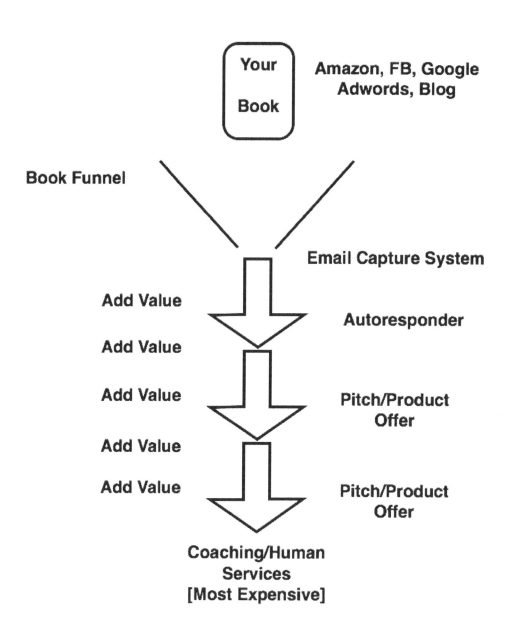

On the same note, Amazon only ranks the kindle sales of your book. Physical copies don't register on you Amazon sales ranking. The money still comes in, but when going for that best seller status, that's secondary.

That's why we lower the price to $0.99 cents. Under that pricing, you only earn 35% royalties. If you want the beloved, "best seller title", then you have to be willing to sacrifice sales price initially. Once you're at Stephen King and J.K. Rowling status, then you can launch at inflated full price...yuss!!!!

So how many sales does it take to become a best seller and for how long do you have to maintain #1 status to officially be called an amazon best seller?

These are two great questions, which don't have a definite answer. Depending on what category you post your book in on Amazon has a lot to do with competition. If Oprah Winfrey is launching a book in your category on the same, you're screwed. But...if you're writing about vegan dog food, (an up and coming niche) I think you would be safe as long as you launch with the technique I described previously.

As for the how long do you have to maintain #1, that one has many gurus and experts conflicting. Some say 2 weeks. That's rather drastic if you're in a niche of high competition. I hit best seller and maintained it for 2 days on my second book. I took a screen shot of the ranking for proof and called myself best seller.

Sales dwindled down, and shot back up, and then later found their medium. If you just touch #1 for a few hours, take a screen shot, tell your fans you hit number one, but I wouldn't call myself a best selling author yet.

The Amazon Orange Flag. When you hit number one and have Amazon on your side for 2-3 days they put an orange flag that says best seller on it. Once you achieve that, I think it's okay to call yourself a best seller. It takes some work and dedication, but it's definitely worth it, in the clout that it has given me. I've earned paid speaking and performing gigs of all kinds. I do a lot for free, if there's a chance to capture leads or sell from the stage. I have a lot of little tricks on that, however, that's a subject for a different book.

If you want more info, secret tips, and a free gift you can click the link here:

http://bit.ly/expertinroom.

Now let's get back to wrapping up. In the next chapter we talk about the whole process in an overview. Now that you have the skills and the know how, we'll take an aerial view to put it all together. See you there.

Chapter 10
The Book Funnel Overview

So here we are, gang. I'm glad yo made it here, and that shows me that you are serious about improving your business and life by adding a book to your prospect pipeline. Yes, you can make thousands to millions in royalties. Yes you can make a difference by finally pursuing that lifelong goal of writing a book. Everyone should write at least one book.

All that is fine and dandy, but a book can open up way opportunities in your networking, hourly rate, brand, and the expansion of e-products in "You Corp". Yes, "You Corp" is your brand and company whether or not you incorporate. You can sell your services, digital information products, books, tee shirts, coffee mugs, and more.

It all starts with a book. You can get speaking engagements, collect leads while you sleep, and automate everything. You do the work once and your book goes out there in digital space marching like a little soldier for you. The more the soldiers in your army, the better. Get it? Good.

Using amazon tags, your Facebook fan page, twitter, blog, Google Adword, or whatever method of traffic assistance, you drive searchers looking for information about your niche. They find your book and either download it instantly on Kindle, or buy the physical copy and wait the 5 days to receive it. This is top level of your funnel. See pic on the next page.

Also, at the top of your funnel is the client that walks in your office. You hand them a book, signed by none other than you, published or best selling author. Either way, each reader is already on your side. They believe in your and somewhat trust you. They read your book and see you point of view. If they can afford your services, they buy right away from a person they know who has put a lot of work into what they do...an accomplished master in your respective field.

They enter your funnel, and if they don't buy right away in your office, they go down the funnel and up the "value ladder".

Every few days, by method of the email autoresponder, you send them value packed messages: tips, tricks, hacks, wisdom, stories. Every four or five emails you pitch them on some of your other value packed products.

A percentage buys and continue to buy each week, month, quarter until they ultimately want your most expensive product: your human services.

Of course there will always, be the tire kickers, but this system pre-qualifies them automatically. Only your raving fans and people who respect the info you're giving them will stay on your list and continue to follow you. All you have to do is give valuable content, and have products available...no matter what the niche.

Royalties roll in, leads roll in, and ultimately sales roll in, meanwhile your brand instantly grows and gains instant leverage for raising your prices and scoring you new jobs and opportunities where there weren't any before.

So, I think the choice is obvious by now. It's not should you get started, or how can you get started. It's when?

Are you ready to embark on an amazing journey, that only goes up? Check out some of the opportunities and gifts in the next chapter and we can decide from there. See you there!

Chapter 11
Done for You Publishing

So you're in. You realize the benefits for you to publish a book and add it to your sales funnel...but...you think you don't have time. I already described my method for people who don't like to write or don't have time to write.

If you are still skeptical about doing it by yourself, then I have a few gifts for you. I have my exact, step by step plan that I used to write a book every two months last year. It's the same organized organizational structure that I teach in my publishing seminars and Turnkey Self Publishing Video Training system.

I also have another gift for you. If you are a speaker, I also include in the book bonus area a **Marketing From the Stage Checklist**, which I pulled from my course "Marketing from the Stage". It is a course that teaches how to Sell when giving a presentation in front of people. The Modules are Goal Setting, Superstar Speaker in

3 Days, Compelling Speaking and Handling Audience, Marketing From the Stage, How to Fill the Room, with bonus Modules: 6 Ways to Eliminate Stage Fright, and Marketing and Webinars. It runs about $197 dollars by itself.

Inside is also information on my full Turkey Self-Publishing Video Training System and if you still are skeptical. There is also a free consultation if you are interested in full book publishing services or...getting started yourself. You have nothing to lose, and everything to gain.

So claim your book bonuses here:

http://bit.ly/expertinroom

Your business and future author self will thank you. If you have any questions, please feel free to contact me at contact@capcorpus.com. I answer all my emails, even if it takes a week. I usually follow up pretty quickly within a day, but sometimes I am backed up a bit, but will do my best to reply quickly.

I hope this book has put value in your life, inspiration in you soul, and a plan of action in your brain. Get out there and become the Expert in the Room!

About the Author

Christopher Robin Roel, 5 time best selling author, lives in South Texas with his family. He runs his Brazilian Martial Arts and Dance Studio, while guest speaking on anti-bullying and confidence building in children. He publishes books for his clients, does seminars on self-publishing and has digital home training courses in publishing, time management, outsourcing, digital product creation, blogging for profit, Youtube live profiting, selling from the stage and more. Reach out to Christopher at contact@capcorpus.com

And don't forget to claim your book bonuses at:

http://bit.ly/expertinroom

Made in the USA
Columbia, SC
21 May 2018